21st CENTURY LIVES
SOAP STARS

Debbie Foy

WAYLAND

First published in 2009 by Wayland

Copyright © Wayland 2009

Wayland
338 Euston Road
London NW1 3BH

Wayland Australia
Level 17/207 Kent Street
Sydney, NSW 2000

Senior editor: Camilla Lloyd
Designer: Simon Burrough
Picture researcher: Diana Morris

Picture Acknowledgments: The author and publisher would like to thank the following for allowing their pictures to be reproduced in this publication: Cover: Rex Features; Don Arnold/Film Magic/ Getty Images: 4, Don Arnold/FM/Getty Images: 11, Don Arnold/Wire Image/Getty Images: 5 © BBC: 13, 17, Gareth Cattermole/Getty Images: 20, David Fisher/Rex Features: 8, 16, 18, 19, Getty Images: 9, ITV/Rex Features: 1, 7, 15, 21, Lindey Parnaby/Getty Images: 6, Rex Features: 12, Ben Stansall/Getty Images: 14, Serge Thomann/Getty Images: 10.

British Library Cataloguing in Publication Data:
Foy, Debbie
    Soap stars. - (21st century lives)
    1. Television actors and actresses - Biography - Juvenile
    literature 2. Television soap operas - Juvenile literature
    I. Title
    791.4'5'028'0922

ISBN: 978 0 7502 5689 6

Printed in China

Wayland is a division of Hachette Children's Books, an Hachette UK company

www.hachette.co.uk

Contents

Ada Nicodemou
Home and Away

Ada arrives at the Annual TV Week Logie Awards in Melbourne, Australia, May 2008.

Real name: Ada Nicodemou

Date and place of birth: 14 May 1977, Sydney, Australia

Background: Ada's parents are both Greek-Cypriots who emigrated to Australia before she was born. Ada attended drama and dance schools from the age of nine and had her first break in television when she was thirteen.

Soap character: Leah Patterson-Baker (Leah Poulos) in *Home and Away.*

Character's key moments: Leah arrived in Summer Bay after running away on the day of her wedding! She has had several dramatic episodes including acting as a surrogate mum for her friend Sally's baby, falling off a cliff and preparing to emigrate to America with her husband, only to find that he had been killed there on an abseiling trip.

Awards or achievements: Ada has been nominated for five Logie Awards; three Gold nominations and two Silver. She won the reality show *Dancing With The Stars* in 2005, with her partner, professional dancer Aric Yegudkin.

Something you might not know about her: In 1999, just before she joined *Home and Away*, Ada appeared in the film *The Matrix* starring Keanu Reeves.

❝ I must admit, I'm a bit of a perfectionist. I'm not really that good at anything, but I work really hard at things. I love dancing and winning *Dancing With The Stars* was great. That kind of dancing is so technical and it doesn't come easily ... We worked on the dance routines for so many hours – but if you asked me to do a tango now I could never do it! ❞

Interview with Ada by Kate Minogue, *Good Health & Medicine*, January 2008

Ada Nicodemou stars as the chatty, big-hearted Leah Patterson-Baker in the Australian soap opera *Home and Away*. One of the soap's favourite characters, Leah arrived in Summer Bay having left her fiancée at the altar. Coming from a traditional Greek background, her parents had arranged the wedding for her, but by the time the big day came Leah realised she wasn't in love with the man she was to marry.

Ada's acting career started when she was very young. At the age of nine and living with her parents in Sydney, Australia, she enrolled at a talent school and then later with a dance show group. After joining these groups, Ada was spotted by a casting agent and has worked in television ever since.

At the age of 13 Ada auditioned for *Home and Away*, but lost out to another girl for the part. However, the audition led to Ada being offered work on the show as an extra which gave Ada an insight into how a television series works behind the scenes and proved to be a valuable experience for later in her career.

Ada is pictured here with Tim Campbell, the actor who played her beloved husband Dan.

When Ada was 15 she auditioned for a new show called *Heartbreak High*. A year later she was called back to do a 12-week stint on the show but she ended up staying for three years. At the same time, Ada was also juggling her school studies with another role in a show called *Police Rescue*. Her acting work took up so much of her time that Ada completed Year 12 (her final year at school) by correspondence. The school would post the work to her, she would complete it inbetween studying her scripts, and then post it back to the school for marking.

Ada studied tourism at college which led to a job as an events co-ordinator, but at the age of 21 she returned to television, appearing in a show called *Breakers*. In 2000 Ada joined *Home and Away*. The cast of *Home and Away* get up at 6am and sometimes shoot scenes for 12 hours a day! Some of Ada's storylines have been very emotional and gruelling, such as when Leah's husband Dan was killed. But Leah is a very strong character and will continue to thrive bringing up her son VJ and running the Diner.

"As a kid I remember watching *Home and Away* and really wanting to join the show. Mum drove me to the auditions, but there were so many other girls there! I did go for a role but missed out. So now that I am here, I really feel I've come full circle and am back where I belong."

Ada Nicodemou,
http://www.seven.com.au/homeandaway

Jack P. Shepherd
Coronation Street

Jack was awarded the title Best Bad Boy at the Inside Soap Awards, September 2008.

" It's always the little old ladies who have a go at me. Younger people think David is great but the grannies attack me with their handbags. "

Jack P. Shepherd on soap fans' reactions to his character, *The Sun*

Real name: Jack Peter Shepherd

Date and place of birth: 14 January 1988, Leeds, England

Background: He was born and brought up in Leeds by mum Janet who is an estate agent and his dad Peter who works for the local council. Jack has an older brother Tom and an older sister Amy. He joined a theatre summer school at the age of ten and has had acting work ever since.

Soap character: David Platt in *Coronation Street*.

Character's key moments: David Platt has been involved in many of the soap's most dramatic storylines. One of his most memorable was when he pushed his mother Gail down the stairs, stepped over her at the bottom and ran off down the street! After his mother finds out that it was her own son who pushed her, David goes on a rampage along the street smashing up cars and causing mayhem!

Awards or achievements: In 2007 and 2008 he won Best Bad Boy at the Inside Soap Awards and in 2008 he won Best Villain at the British Soap Awards.

Something you might not know about him: David admits that he has a special way of getting into character for his moody scenes. He stays up late the night before so that he has dark rings under his eyes, then he tilts his head down and looks up at the character he is talking to – this makes his eyes look really evil!

A scene from Coronation Street *in which Charlie Stubbs gets his revenge on David Platt for trying to break up his relationship with Maria Sutherland.*

If there were an award for worst teen on the screen David Platt would surely win it. There has been lots of turmoil and upset in his life, including his parents' divorce and his mother's new boyfriend kidnapping the whole family! David has changed from happy child to a manipulative, sour-faced teenager who will stop at nothing to get what he wants. David has already spent time in a Young Offenders Institution, attempted to commit suicide to ruin his sister's wedding and almost killed his niece by storing drugs in one of her dolls! Meet David Platt - the true soap baddie ... expertly played by Jack P. Shepherd.

Jack's upbringing was a far cry from David's troubled childhood. Even when he was very young Jack was a great film fan, sometimes watching up to five films a day. Inspired by the actors he saw on screen, Jack realised that he would like to act but it was thanks to his mum that this ambition was realised. During the summer holidays when Jack was ten his mum was desperate to get him away from his Playstation and doing something worthwhile. She enrolled him at a summer school hosted by Stage 84 Drama School based in Bradford. It paid off, and Jack won his first audition for the series *Where The Heart Is* a week later.

Small parts in other dramas followed and in due course, Jack was spotted by Granada Television as a potential replacement for Thomas Ormson who had played the role of David Platt since he was born. At the audition, Jack made an immediate impression on the Granada bosses and they offered him a three-month contract to join the cast of *Coronation Street*. Though Jack has a busy schedule, filming around four episodes of the soap a week, he still finds time to keep up his theatre appearances and since he began on *Coronation Street* he has starred in *West Side Story* at the Edinburgh Fringe and in the musical *Oliver!* at the Alhambra theatre in Bradford.

Though Jack is dedicated and ambitious, he has no desire to leave the cobbled streets of the Weatherfield for the forseeable future, and enjoys playing the soap villain so much that he hopes the show's writers keep writing wicked antics for him! Keep your eyes peeled for David Platt – and be glad he doesn't live on *your* street!

"Keep an eye on David Platt. I think Jack P. Shepherd's a terrific young actor. There's this wonderful dark humour about the character that's been emerging very subtly over the last year – and we're really going to go places with that character. It's one of those great stories where it's going to have ripples right through the community."

Kieran Roberts, controller of Drama for ITV Productions, www.manchestereveningnews.co.uk, 14 March 2007

Kara Tointon
EastEnders

Real name: Kara Louise Tointon

Date and place of birth: August 5 1983, Basildon, Essex, England

Background: Kara is the eldest daughter of Carol and Ken. She is dyslexic and wasn't very academic at school, but was very creative and drawn to activities such as gymnastics, dancing and drama. Kara and her sister Hannah were brought up in Southend, Essex.

Soap character: Dawn Swann in *EastEnders*.

Character's key moments: Since joining *EastEnders* in 2005, Kara has been involved in some of the show's biggest storylines. She gave birth to her daughter Summer after being kidnapped and conned her neighbours out of money to pay for an operation – which turned out to be cosmetic surgery!

Awards or achievements: Nominated for Most Popular Actress at National Television Awards 2007. Also voted Sexiest Female at the British Soap Awards 2007. Kara also won the Sport Relief version of *Strictly Come Dancing* in March 2008, partnering Mark Ramprakash.

Something you might not know about her: Kara's sister Hannah is also a soap star and previously played the role of Katy Fox in *Hollyoaks.*

The annual British Soap Awards is the chance for hardworking soap stars to dress up and let their hair down.

" The first thing I ever did [on TV] was when I was 12 and I had a non-speaking part. It was at Sonia Fowler's birthday party and I was just at the back eating crisps. It was literally a second on screen but my mum has still got a video of it. "

Kara Tointon on her first role in *EastEnders* as an extra, www.karatointon.net.

Kara Tointon is a young woman with a dazzling career ahead of her. Playing the role of loudmouth, flirtatious Dawn Swann launched her into a major TV soap role and ambitious Kara won't be looking back.

A creative and energetic child, Kara took speech and drama lessons and entered local music festivals to perform poetry recitals. Her first experience of acting was at the age of seven performing in *The Sound of Music* in her local theatre in Southend. After joining the prestigious Sylvia Young Agency at the age of 12 her first acting part on television was as an extra in *EastEnders*.

During her teens Kara starred in adverts for Pringles and McDonalds, and at the age of 16 she decided to follow her creative streak and began to study interior design at college. Acting was always there in the background and soon after starting college, she left to take on a role in Channel 4's hit TV show *Teachers*. Since then she has appeared in numerous TV shows including *Mile High* and *Dream Team*. In 2005 she successfully auditioned for the part of Dawn Swann and her new role propelled Kara to a new level of fame!

Drama seems to follow Dawn Swann everywhere she goes. Dawn arrived in Albert Square announcing that she was a model, but took a job as a barmaid to make ends meet. She conned money out of the neighbours to pay for plastic surgery and embarked on an affair with a married man, in which she fell pregnant and ended up being kidnapped! Dawn found love again but the day before her wedding her fiancée, Jase, was murdered.

In reality Kara's life is a million miles away from the troubled Dawn. Her family are very close and she describes her younger sister Hannah as her best friend. She is a trained dancer, specialising in ballet, jazz and tap and in her spare time she enjoys painting, swimming and skiing. She has achieved a good work-life balance and has a sensible head on her young shoulders. This ambitious young woman's career can only get better and better.

Dawn Swann is a charmer and knows how to get what she wants from life!

"Kara arrives to meet the *Sugar* crew dressed in her mum's shoes from the '80s. She's sweet, smiley and very down to earth. And she admits she loves her fake-tan evenings so much, she can't even think of moving in with her boyfriend any time soon! Now THAT'S our kind of girl."

Sugar magazine, April 2006

Kym Valentine
Neighbours

Kym Valentine celebrating her return to Neighbours *at a party hosted by Channel 10 Television in Melbourne, Australia in July 2007.*

" I am hugely loyal to the show and I'm ready to go back and do what I love. "

Kym Valentine on her return to Neighbours, November 2007

Actor's name: Kym Valentine

Date and place of birth: 24 May 1977, Blacktown, Sydney, Australia

Background: Kym is Maltese-Australian. She has been acting, singing and dancing since the age of five, when she made her debut appearing in a McDonalds advert.

Soap character: Libby Kennedy, daughter of Karl and Susan Kennedy in *Neighbours*.

Character's key moments: Libby defied death in a motorbike crash and during the birth of her son, Ben. Her husband Drew was killed in a horse riding accident not long after her mother Susan Kennedy suffered amnesia following a blow to her head.

Awards or achievements: Kym is an ambassador for Taylor & Khoo, an organisation that supports orphans and disadvantaged people in Cambodia.

Something you might not know about her: Kym's favourite film is *Gone With The Wind* and says if she wasn't an actress, she would be a director or a singer.

Kym Valentine's *Neighbours* career began at the age of 17. She devoted ten years of her life to the show before taking a break in 2004 to pursue stage work, but such is her passion for the show that she returned to *Neighbours* in 2007 after a three-year break. Kym had been acting and appearing in shows since childhood, but at the age of 15 she won her first big part in a short-lived comedy series called *My Two Wives*, where she played a character called Lisa Kennedy. Coincidentally, her next role was also as a Kennedy but this time it was Libby Kennedy in *Neighbours* – the feisty and politically-minded daughter of Karl and Susan Kennedy.

In 2004 Kym took a break from television to pursue her theatre interests and won the lead role of Frances 'Baby' Houseman for the musical production *Dirty Dancing: The Classic Story on Stage*. When the production transferred from Sydney to London, Kym stayed in Australia to pursue her other great interest, music.

Kym had been a regular live singer in Melbourne pubs with the band Feedback, but since 2006 she has been performing weekly at *The Official Neighbours Bingo and Karaoke Bash* in which fans are able to watch their favourite *Neighbours* stars from past and present perform live.

Kym's character, Libby, is a passionate and intelligent woman. After a stint on the *Erinsborough News*, Libby followed in her mother's footsteps and began teaching. Libby has had a troubled love life, falling for bad boy Darren Stark, then marrying the love of her life, Drew Kirk. After a terrible motorbike accident Libby thought she would not be able to have children, but against the odds she fell pregnant. Her son Ben's birth was traumatic enough but shortly after this Drew was killed in a tragic horse riding accident. After a period away, Libby is back and hoping to rebuild her life in Erinsborough. Let's hope she can be lucky in love next time.

Kym Valentine on the red carpet at the Australian television industry awards (otherwise known as the Logie Awards) 2008.

"Kym Valentine rejoined the show in 2007. She is a wonderful girl and just like a daughter to me."

Alan Fletcher, who plays Libby's screen father, Dr Karl Kennedy, www.thefounder.co.uk

11

Lacey Turner
EastEnders

Lacey at the Bafta TV Awards in 2007.

Real name: Lacey Amelia Turner

Date and place of birth: 28 March 1988, Hendon, London, England

Background: Born to parents Bev and Les, Lacey is the eldest of three children. She and her two younger sisters grew up in Hertfordshire, close to Elstree Studios where *EastEnders* is filmed.

Soap character: Stacey Branning (previously Slater) in *EastEnders*.

Character's key moments: Stacey has been involved in many high profile storylines including abortion, drug abuse, mental illness and an affair with her husband's father!

Awards or achievements: British Soap Awards 2006, Best Actress; British Soap Awards 2007, Best Dramatic Performance; National Television Awards 2007, Most Popular Actress; Inside Soap 2007, Best Actress and Best Couple (with Charlie Clements); British Soap Awards 2008, Best Storyline. These are accompanied by a whole host of nominations for other awards.

Something you might not know about her: Since she has gained celebrity status Lacey has revealed that she was bullied while at stage school, by children who called her 'geeky'. So instead she attended a local comprehensive and took dance, singing and acting lessons outside of school.

> **❝I love everything about her. She's boisterous and a loud mouth. Everything people can't and won't say, she says and does. She gets on with her life and says and does what she wants and doesn't care. I think she's great.❞**

Lacey Turner on her character, Stacey Branning, *Celebs on Sunday Magazine, Sunday Mirror,* 14 March 2008

Bradley and Stacey Branning's big day was aired on 1 November 2007 in a one-hour special episode.

Stacey Branning is Walford's number one minx. Played by the brilliant award-winning young actress Lacey Turner, we wait with bated breath to find out what scrapes Stacey gets herself into next!

Lacey Turner has achieved her dream – to play a starring role in *EastEnders*; a dream she has had ever since listening to the show being filmed from her bedroom window that overlooked Elstree Studios when she was a child.

She attended the famous Sylvia Young Theatre School at the age of ten, but left after a year. Lacey took singing, dancing and drama lessons outside school instead and attended the local girls' comprehensive. Lacey's first acting job was in an advertisement for Haribo sweets at the age of 12. She performed in several theatre productions before auditioning for *EastEnders* at the age of 15. Lacey actually auditioned for a different role, but was given the part of the feisty, troublesome Stacey Slater instead. She began work on *EastEnders* in 2004 – the day after she left school – and Lacey was thrilled to be working alongside the people that she had always admired.

Stacey was introduced to the show as Stacey Slater. Her character has developed into a tough, stubborn, fiery and determined young woman with a troubled past. Her dad died when she was young and her mum is coping with mental illness. Though Stacey has had several troubled relationships, in 2006 she married Bradley Branning, played by Charlie Clements. Her affair with Bradley's father Max Branning and its repercussions has been one of the most talked-about episodes in *EastEnders* history.

Since working on *EastEnders* Lacey has received many awards and numerous nominations. She is one of the show's most popular characters and though she has expressed a desire to explore avenues outside of soap, we know this brilliantly-played character will go down in soap legend.

"She hit the screen with such confidence. This girl is just going to get better and better."

Kathleen Hutchison, executive producer of *EastEnders*, *The Guardian* website, 27 November 2004

Roxanne Pallett
Emmerdale

Roxanne arrives at the British Soap Awards to a hoard of photographers wanting to take her picture!

" I'm so excited about what's in store for Jo! I never stop trying to evolve her character. When I'm out I always watch people and use that as research. I know Jo inside out and I have been lucky that the writers have included me in her progression. "

Roxanne Pallett on her character, AOL Entertainment, 14 January 2008

Real name: Roxanne Pallett

Date and place of birth: 26 December 1982, Carlisle, Cumbria, England

Background: Roxanne was brought up by her mother and grandmother in Carlisle and attended the local primary and secondary schools. She completed a degree in Media and Cultural Studies at Liverpool John Moores University.

Soap character: Jo Sugden (previously Stiles) in *Emmerdale*.

Character's key moments: Jo made a big impression in 2005 on her arrival in *Emmerdale* as the new veterinary receptionist. With a reputation as a bit of a 'maneater', Jo caused Andy and Katie Sugden's marriage to break up. Jo subsequently married Andy in 2008 while he was in prison for setting fire to his stepmother's cottage!

Awards or achievements: Roxanne has been nominated for Sexiest Female at the British Soap Awards in 2006, 2007 and 2008. At the 2008 British Soap Awards she was also nominated for Best Actress.

Something you might not know about her: Roxanne has a beautiful deep red rose named after her, called *The Roxanne Pallett Rose!*

You could say that Roxanne Pallett and her *Emmerdale* character Jo Sugden share many qualities. Both of them are confident, bright and sassy; they both know what they want from life and are prepared to work hard to get it!

Roxanne did not attend theatre school but had an ordinary upbringing in Cumbria. In her early twenties she was part of an all-girl band called Urban Angel. The band was on the brink of winning two record deals, but then lost out on both at the last minute. Roxanne felt defeated, but picked herself up and decided that she was going to make all the hard work she had put into the band pay off somehow!

She met an agent through a contact in the music business and within three months of the band splitting up, Roxanne was attending auditions for some of the most popular shows on television.

Roxanne's original *Emmerdale* audition was for the part of Jasmine, the vicar's niece, but the writers of the show liked her so much they wrote the part of Jo Stiles for her.

In August 2005 Roxanne joined the cast of *Emmerdale*. She has appeared on the cover of several magazines and her profile is increasing. In 2006 she took part in the reality show *Soapstar Superstar* and admits that a career in singing is something she would still like to pursue.

Would Roxanne's *Emmerdale* character revel in this kind of attention? Jo Sugden's arrival in *Emmerdale* hit the village like a bombshell. Though basically good at heart, Jo has blackmailed, deceived and spread gossip. She stole Katie Sugden's husband from under her nose! She currently lives at Butler's Farm with her husband Andy and his daughter. But how long will minxy Jo be content with the domestic life…?

"She's used to working hard to get what she wants. It's how she's learned to be so manipulative. She totally focuses on herself and her needs – she doesn't take other peoples' feelings into consideration at all."

Roxanne Pallett on her character in *Emmerdale*, *What's On TV*, 2007

In 2006 Jo was invited to stay at Butler's Farm with Andy Sugden (second from the left) and his wife Katie (far left), but flirtatious Jo wrecked havoc in the Sugden household.

Patsy Palmer
EastEnders

Patsy currently lives in Brighton, East Sussex with her husband and three children.

Real name: Julie Harris

Date and place of birth: 26 May 1972, Bethnal Green, London, England

Background: She was brought up by her mother in east London, alongside her two elder brothers. Patsy attended acting classes outside of regular school hours as her mother could not afford to send her to drama school. She starred in a West End production of *Joseph and his Amazing Technicolour Dreamcoat* at the age of six.

Soap character: Bianca Jackson in *EastEnders*.

Character's key moments: Bianca has been involved in many dramatic storylines, including affairs, bereavements and abortion. She left Walford in 1999 to live in Manchester, but in April 2008 Bianca returned to Albert Square with four children in tow. Bianca became famous for her catchphrase 'Rickaaaaaay!' which she used to yell at Ricky Butcher when she was married to him.

Awards or achievements: Patsy was the first soap actress ever to be nominated for Best Actress at the Royal Television Awards, 1998; awarded Best Actress at the Soap Awards, 2000.

Something you might not know about her: Her stage name, Patsy Palmer, is actually her real-life mother's name.

> ❝ I'm delighted to welcome Patsy Palmer home to *EastEnders*. Bianca is one of the most popular characters the show has ever had. Millions grew up with her and, like the audience I can't wait to see her back in the show. ❞
>
> **Diederick Santer, executive producer of *EastEnders*, on Bianca's return to Albert Square, www.timesonline.co.uk, 29 October 2007**

In April 2008 Bianca Jackson and her four children, Whitney, Liam, Tiffany and Morgan, made a dramatic return to Walford.

Patsy Palmer is best known for her role as the feisty Bianca Jackson, one of the most popular characters in *EastEnders*' history. Bianca made her first appearance in the show in 1993 but six years later Patsy Palmer decided to leave the character of Bianca and *EastEnders* behind to bring up a family and pursue other interests. In April 2008 the much-loved Bianca Jackson made a highly publicised return to Albert Square.

It was Patsy's mother who first spotted her acting talent and enrolled her at the Anna Scher Acting School in Islington, London. She appeared on the West End stage at an early age and was in the popular children's drama show, *Grange Hill*, in 1986 and 1987.

In 1993 she was cast in the role of stroppy Bianca Jackson in *EastEnders*. She was a popular character from the start and her relationship with Ricky Butcher, played by Sid Owen, captivated millions of fans. The marriage of Bianca and Ricky in 1997 drew 22 million viewers — one of the biggest soap audiences ever!

Patsy left *EastEnders* in 1999 to work on various stage and TV projects. She starred in the one-woman musical *Tell Me On A Sunday* and in a West End run of *Mum's the Word*. She also had a lead role in the UK tour of the musical *Steppin' Out*. In 2001 she starred in a detective drama series *McCready and Daughter* and she released a number of popular fitness videos and DVDs. In 2005 Patsy took part in BBC's *Strictly Come Dancing* to raise money for Children in Need. In 2007 she published her biography *All of Me* in which she describes how she battled bullying and other problems to find fame. In addition to acting she has recently set up her own company, Palmer Cutler, selling beauty products.

Historically Patsy's character Bianca has featured in many dramatic storylines, including family problems, affairs and abortion. Her return to Walford in 2008 was similarly high profile and dramatic, arriving with four children by different fathers. Bianca's former husband — the long-suffering Ricky — has also arrived back in Walford, so tune in to the show and watch out for fireworks!

"I'm really excited about rejoining the cast and working with old friends again. I can't wait to explore what Bianca has been doing with her life and seeing what she is going to get up to next."

Patsy Palmer on her return to Walford, BBC press release, www.bbc.co.uk/pressoffice/ pressreleases/stories, 29 October 2007

Scott Maslen

EastEnders

Scott plays Jack Branning, a smooth operator who has caused quite a stir in Walford since he arrived in 2007.

" I call him amoral; neither good nor bad. He gets what he wants out of a situation but that isn't necessarily just a selfish thing. He's not an evil character, but if there are people that are threatening him, his business or his family, he will do whatever he needs to do to eliminate the problem. "

Scott Maslen on his character, Jack Branning, www.bbc.co.uk/eastenders, 13 December 2007

Actor's name: Scott Alexander Maslen

Date and place of birth: 25 June 1972, London, England

Background: Scott's parents separated when Scott was seven and his mother Janet brought up Scott and his older sister Suzy. He enjoyed school but played the part of the joker and did not pay much attention to studying. At 16 he joined the Royal Marines, but a broken foot cut short his career and at the age of 18 he embarked on a modelling career.

Soap character: Jack Branning, the younger brother of Max Branning and Carol Jackson.

Character's key moments: Jack's arrival in Albert Square caused quite a stir among several residents. Though Jack helped Phil track down his daughter, the feud between Jack and Phil is ongoing as Jack blackmailed Phil into selling him the car lot. His stormy on-off relationship with Ronnie Mitchell resulted in Ronnie punching Jack when she discovered he had been dating someone else!

Awards or achievements: Scott was nominated for Sexiest Male at the British Soap Awards 2008.

Something you might not know about him: Scott is a huge West Ham football fan and a keen fisherman!

He's a rogue, he's flash, he's successful and he's on the Square! When Jack Branning arrived in Walford for Bradley and Stacey's wedding his impact was like a tornado. Since his appearance in 2007 Jack has conned Phil Mitchell out of his car lot business and muscled in on his brother Max's relationship with his wife Tanya.

Scott Maslen was brought up in Woolwich. He had a short-lived career in the Royal Marines before he was spotted on a Miami beach by the famous American fashion photographer, Bruce Weber. Before long Scott was modelling for famous designers such as Versace and Armani all over the world and appearing on the front covers of top fashion magazines such as *Vogue*.

After five years of modelling Scott returned to London to pursue his acting ambitions and enrolled at the Guildhall School of Music and Drama. In 2000 he was offered the part of Jamie in the TV series *Lock, Stock…* He appeared briefly in episodes of *Peak Practice* and *Heartbeat*. In 2002 Scott landed the role of Detective Superintendent Phil Hunter in *The Bill*. It was this role that launched Scott into the world of soap celebrity. Controversy was sparked in 2007 when Scott was offered the role of Jack Branning in *EastEnders*, since it was the first time that an actor had been poached from one popular soap opera by another.

Ex-policeman Jack Branning is a shady character with a murky past, but his good looks, charisma and sharp business mind means that he has quickly established himself in the Square in business and in his personal life. However, he has made many enemies along the way, so watch out for Jack Branning!

Scott gets a kiss from Rita Simons (right), who plays Roxy Mitchell and Barbara Windsor (left) who plays Peggy Mitchell.

"Our flat in Blackheath, south London, looked out over a garden where we could see Glenda Jackson, Oliver Reed and Alan Bates shooting the film *Women in Love*. Scott was only small but who knows?"

Scott Maslen's father, John Maslen speculating on how his son caught the acting bug, *The Mirror*, 8 November 2007

Samia Smith
Coronation Street

Although Samia attends lots of glitzy award shows, in reality she prefers quiet nights in.

" Being an actor, it is amazing to get to act all year round. I'm very lucky indeed to be in such an amazing programme. **"**

Samia Smith on her role in
Coronation Street,
www.manchestereveningnews.co.uk
3 December 2007

Real name: Samia Maxine Smith (previously Ghadie)

Date and place of birth: 13 July 1982, Eccles, Salford, England

Background: Samia grew up in Salford with her mother, a former cabaret artist and her father, a former diver of French-Lebanese descent. She has an older brother, Tariq.

Soap character: Maria Connor (previously Sutherland) in *Coronation Street.*

Character's key moments: One of Maria's most dramatic scenes was when she saved David Platt from being drowned in the bath by her then-boyfriend, Charlie Stubbs!

Awards or achievements: Won the award for Best Storyline at 2007 British Soap Awards. Nominated for Sexiest Female at British Soap Awards 2007 and 2008.

Something you might not know about her: Samia's hobby is baking cakes and she claims that her lemon drizzle cake is the best!

Samia Smith who plays the character Maria Connor has her feet firmly under the table at *Coronation Street.*

Samia went to drama lessons from the age of six and also modelled children's clothes in catalogues. When she was eight she appeared in *Coronation Street* as an extra, but did not get a speaking part on TV until she was 11, when she appeared in an episode of *Cracker.* She went on to play small parts in various TV dramas such as *Doctor's, Heartbeat* and *Children's Ward.* Her big break came while she was studying for her A-levels. Samia was picked to star in the British film *There's Only One Jimmy Grimble* alongside notable actors such as Robert Carlyle, Ray Winstone and Gina McKee.

In 2000 Samia auditioned for and won the role of Maria Sutherland in Coronation Street, succeeding over ex-'Hear' Say singer Suzanne Shaw and Girls Aloud singer Kimberley Walsh who also auditioned for the part!

Maria Sutherland entered the show in May 2000 as a dowdy kennel maid, but over the past few years she has blossomed into one of *Coronation Street's* most glamorous and popular young women. The sister of Kirk Sutherland, Maria works as a hairdresser in Audrey Roberts's hair salon. She has had a troubled love-life including her past relationship with the soft-hearted mechanic Tyrone Dobbs and her liaison with bad boy Charlie Stubbs! David Platt also had an infatuation with Maria which resulted in a show-down when Charlie attacked him.

When the good-looking Liam Connor arrived on the street in 2007, Maria fell for him in a big way. They married in 2008 but Maria gave birth to a still-born baby – a scene that Samia found very challenging to play since her own mother had been through the same experience many years ago. However, it appears that poor Maria is destined to be forever unlucky in love. Liam is murdered in October 2008 and it seems that his heart was set on someone else before his death ...

Samia's real life is a far cry from the hectic and dramatic life lead by her character Maria Connor! Samia is happily married and enjoys the quiet life at home with her husband, walking her Maltese terrier, Sonny, and of course, baking her famous lemon drizzle cake!

A scene from Coronation Street *in which Maria and Liam's troubled relationship was only just beginning ...*

"I find the fact that magazines are interested in taking pictures of me really weird because I don't think of myself like that. No-one fancied me at school – if they did they must have been geekier than me, I was a swot."

Samia Smith on her celebrity status, *The Mirror,* 28 November 2007

Other Soap Stars

Jennifer Metcalfe (Mercedes McQueen - Hollyoaks)

Jennifer Metcalfe plays the feisty and confrontational Mercedes McQueen, whose behaviour often gets her into hot water!

Jennifer Metcalfe was born into a working class family in Bradford on 4 September 1985. She is the youngest of six brothers and one sister. Her interest in drama and acting came from watching prime-time dramas in which several local actors performed. Jennifer went to a drama club in Bradford and later she attended a drama school in nearby Leeds, where she studied Performing Arts at GCSE. She then went on to study A-level Dance and Drama and a Health and Fitness degree. She realised that acting was her passion and she went all out to get into the profession.

Jennifer's previous parts include roles in *Emmerdale, Where the Heart Is, Birthday Girl, At Home with the Braithwaites* and *My Parents are Aliens.* Jennifer was thrilled to land the role of Mercedes in *Hollyoaks* in 2006.

Mercedes Maria Theresa Immaculata McQueen has a dangerous streak and is always causing trouble or has some scam on the go. She enjoys taking risks and usually seems to get what she wants. Watch out for the super-confident Mercedes on your screens!

William Roache (Ken Barlow – Coronation Street)

William Patrick Roache is the only living member of *Coronation Street* who was part of the original cast. His first appearance on the soap was in episode one, on 9 December 1960. William was born on 25 April 1932 in Ilkeston, Derbyshire. He intended to study medicine, but in 1953 he was commissioned into the Royal Welsh Fusiliers where he became a captain. He spent five years in the services with postings all over the world.

In 1999 William Roache was awarded the Special Achievement Award at the British Soap Awards for playing the role of Ken Barlow for 40 years. In 2001, he was awarded an MBE (Member of the Order of the British Empire) for his services to television drama.

Ken Barlow was born and bred on the famous cobbles of *Coronation Street*. He was the first resident of the street to go to university. However, Ken has never really achieved professional success and over the years he has had many jobs including teacher, taxi driver and supermarket trolley collector. He has been married numerous times to Valerie Tatlock, Janet Reid and Deirdre Langton (who he has married twice!). He has fathered or step-fathered several children including Deirdre's wayward daughter, Tracey Barlow, who was sent to prison in 2007 for murder! Let's hope that *Coronation Street*'s most famous couple, Deirdre and Ken can stay together and continue to entertain us.

Nick Pickard (Tony Hutchinson - Hollyoaks)

Nick Pickard is *Hollyoaks'* longest serving actor, appearing in the show's first ever episode in October 1995. Nick's real-life brother, John Pickard, plays the role of Tony's half-brother, Dominic Reilly, in the show! The brothers share a flat and help each other to learn their lines.

Nick trained at the famous Sylvia Young Theatre School in London and did plenty of theatrical work before joining the soap, even treading the boards in *Richard II*. In 1987 he played the lead role in a movie called *Mio in the Land of*

Faraway alongside Christopher Lee and Christian Bale. In 1994 he also played minor roles in *Grange Hill* and *EastEnders*, in which he appeared as a young homeless boy who met a grisly end when Phil Mitchell set fire to the car lot! Nick has no plans to leave the most-watched teenage soap opera. His screen character Tony is famous for his many on-off relationships, affairs and engagements. Tony has also had his fair share of heartache, for example when he suffered the cot death of his daughter, Grace and when his good friend Max died.

In 2001 and 2002 Nick Pickard was nominated for Best Comedy Performance at the British Soap Awards.

Kym Ryder (Michelle Connor – Coronation Street)

Kym Ryder was born Kym Gail Marsh on 13 June 1976, in Garswood, Lancashire. The youngest of four children, Kym enjoyed singing and performing. At the age of 13 she appeared on *Richard and Judy* promoting her first single!

On leaving theatre school at 15 Kym took various jobs including work as a receptionist and a shop assistant, but her heart was firmly set on a singing career. In 2000 she attended an audition in Manchester for a TV show called *Popstars*. She was one of the five people selected to form the band Hear'Say. They released a number one song, *Pure and Simple*, and received a great deal of media publicity over the next couple of years.

In 2002 Kym left the band and landed a starring role in the West End musical *Saturday Night Fever*. Bitten by the acting bug she decided to go after other acting roles. After brief appearances in *Doctors* and *Holby City*, in 2006 Kym achieved one of her major ambitions in life and landed a long-term role in *Coronation Street*. Kym plays the character Michelle Connor, a young single mum. She works at the Rovers Return pub and has already managed to alienate the landlady Liz McDonald, who was dismayed when her son Steve fell for the bubbly barmaid.

With tough-cookie Michelle Connor firmly established behind the bar at the Rovers, and a relationship with the landlady's son, it looks as though Kym Ryder is set to be treading the cobbles of *Coronation Street* for the foreseeable future!

Ricky Whittle (Calvin Valentine – Hollyoaks)

Ricky Whittle was born in Oldham, near Manchester. Ricky is a keen sportsman and he represented his country at youth level in football, rugby and athletics. He was scouted by Arsenal and Celtic football teams but his life took a dramatic turn when a string of injuries meant that he could not rely on football for a career. While at university studying a law degree, he started modelling. In 2000 Ricky became the face of Reebok in an advertising campaign.

He auditioned for Sky One's *Dream Team* and won a leading role as Ryan Naysmith. After a freak accident in which he broke his leg so badly he was told he wouldn't run again, Ricky was bed bound for several months. He has since made a full recovery, proving the doctors wrong, and is now back playing football again!

After a stint on *Holby City* Ricky began appearing in *Hollyoaks* in summer 2006, playing the local police constable. Not long after Calvin arrived at *Hollyoaks*, tragedy struck in the Valentine family when their mum was killed in a hit-and-run accident. Since then, Calvin has been fiercely protective of the family. Calvin is a likeable character, witty and intelligent, who wants to do the right thing.

Though Ricky is happy with his soap role, he has said that he would like to test himself in different roles – romance, comedy or action. Keep an eye out for this ambitious actor - who knows where you might see him next?

Index